WOMEN'S EDITION
VOLUME 48

# Easygoing R&B

T0079943

ISBN 978-1-4234-6557-7

HAL•LEONARD®
CORPORATION
7777 W. BLUEMOUND RD. P.O. BOX 13819 MILWAUKEE, WI 53213

Visit Hal Leonard Online at
**www.halleonard.com**

# Easygoing R&B

# Best Thing That Ever Happened to Me

Words and Music by Jim Weatherly

# Feel Like Makin' Love
## Words and Music by Eugene McDaniels

when you're moan - in' sweet _ and low, _____

when you touch _ me, and my feel - ings start _ to show, _____

ooh, _____ that's the time _ I feel like mak - in' love _

_____ to you. _____ Ooh, _____ that's the time _

I feel like mak - in' dreams _ come true. _____ Oh, _ babe. _

**Verse**

_____ 3. In a res - tau - rant hold - in' hands _ by can - dle -

light, _____ while I'm touch - in' you,

want - in' you _ with all _ my might, _____ ooh, _____

_____ that's the time _ I feel like mak - in' love _____ to you. _

**9**

# The First Time Ever I Saw Your Face

**Words and Music by Ewan MacColl**

end     of the skies. _____

2. And the first     time ___

ev - er ___ I   kissed ___     your ___     mouth, ___

I felt ___ the earth _____     move   in my  hand, _____

_____     like  the ___ trem - bling

heart _____     of   a   cap - tive ___   bird _____

that _____     was there _____     at   my ___ com - mand, ___

___     my love.     3. And the first ___ time _____     ev-

er   I   lay ___   with ___  you, ___     I  felt ___ your

heart _____ so close __ to mine, _____

and I knew _____ our joy _____

would fill _____ the earth, ___ and last _____

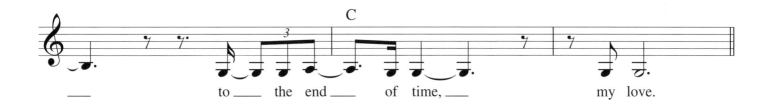

___ to ___ the end ___ of time, ___ my love.

**Outro**

The first __ time ___ ev - er I saw _____

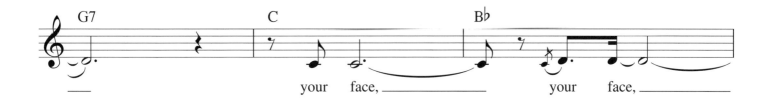

___ your face, _____ your face, _____

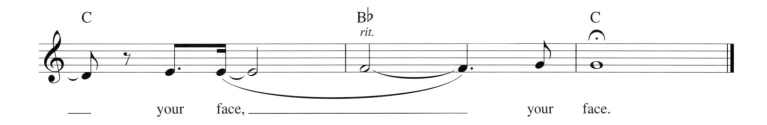

___ your face, _____ your face.

# I Heard It Through the Grapevine

**Words and Music by Norman J. Whitfield and Barrett Strong**

**Chorus**

F7                                C                Gm/C    F/C

yes - ter - day.    Don't you know _ that I    heard it through the grape - vine?

F7              C            Gm/C   F/C     F7

Not much long - er would you be _ mine.     Don't you know _ that I

C             Gm/C     F/C     F7

heard it through the grape - vine?      Ooh, ___ no, ___

C             Gm/C     F/C     F7

___ just a - bout, just a - bout, just a - bout to    lose ___ my mind, _ oh,

Cm                                       3

yes, I am,    oh, ___ yes, I am. _    Ba - by, won't you lis - ten to me?

**Verse**

                            C                        Gm/C     F/C

2. Boy, _ take a good _ look _ at these tears in my eyes.

C    Gm/C   F/C    G                    F7

Boy, _ these tears ___ I can't _ hold _____ in - side. _

C      Gm/C   F/C     C            Gm/C   F/C     G

Los - in' you would end my life, you see, _     be - cause you mean that

much to me. You could -'ve told _____ me your-self

that you love some - bod - y else. _ In - stead I

**Chorus**

heard it through the grape - vine, ooh, _ not much

long - er would you be _ mine. Don't you know _ I

heard it through the grape - vine? _ Ooh, _____

_ just a - bout, just a - bout, just a - bout to lose _____ my mind, _ oh,

**Interlude**

yes, I am. _____ Ah,

ah. _____

**Verse**

3. Say be-lieve half __ of what you see, oh, __ no, __ and none of what you hear. Ba - by, ba - by, I __ can't help __ be - in' con - fused. __ If it's true, __ please, _ ba - by, won't you tell __ __ me, dear? _ Oh, __ do you plan __ to let me go for the oth - er girl you loved be - fore? Don't you know _ that I

**Outro-Chorus**

heard it through the grape - vine? Not much long - - er would you be __ mine. Don't you know _ that I heard it? Yes, I heard it.

*Fadeout*

Ooh, I heard it, heard it, heard it.

# Killing Me Softly with His Song

**Words by Norman Gimbel**
**Music by Charles Fox**

**Verse**

Bbm        Eb9        Ab

1. I heard he sang ___ a good ___ song, ___ I ___ heard he

Dbmaj7        Bbm        Eb9

had a style, ___ and so I came ___ to see ___ him to

Fm        Bbm

lis - ten ___ for a while. ___ And there ___ he was, ___

Eb7        Ab        C7

___ this young ___ boy, a stran - ger to ___ my eyes. ___

**Chorus**

Fm        Bbm7

Strum - min' my pain ___ with his fin - gers, ___

Eb7        Ab        Fm

sing - in' my life ___ with his words. ___ Kill - ing me soft - ly with his ___

Bb7/D        Eb        Db

___ song, kill - ing me soft - ly ___ with his ___ song, tell - in' my whole ___

Ab        Db       3    Gbmaj7

___ life with his ___ words, kill - ing me soft - ly ___

with his song.

**Verse**

Bbm7     Eb9     Ab

2. I felt all flushed _ with fe - ver, _____ em - bar - rassed _

Dbmaj7    Bbm7    Eb7

_ by the _ crowd. _____ I felt he found _ my let - ters and

Fm            Bbm7

read each _ one out ____ loud. _____ I prayed _ that he _

Eb7       Ab     C7

_ would fin - ish, but he just kept ___ right on. _____

𝄋 **Chorus**

Fm            Bbm7

Strum - min' my pain ____ with his fin - gers, _____

Eb7       Ab     Fm

sing - in' my life _ with his words. _ Kill - ing me soft - ly with his _

Bb7/D     Eb     Db

_ song, kill - ing me soft - ly _____ with his ___ song, tell - in' my whole _

**Bridge**

Oh, _____

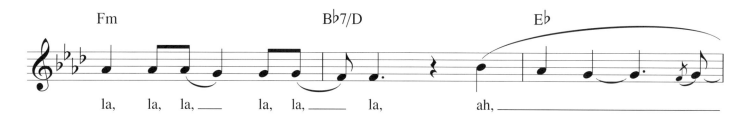

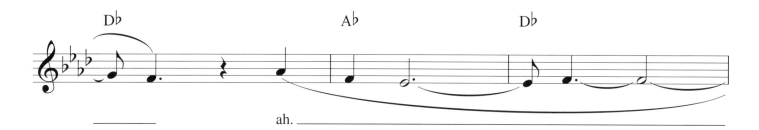

la, la, la, \_\_\_\_ la, la, \_\_\_\_ la, ah, \_\_\_\_

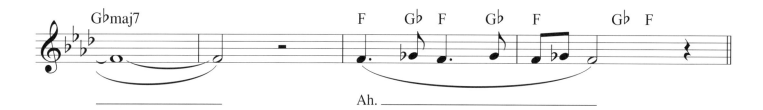

_____ ah. _____

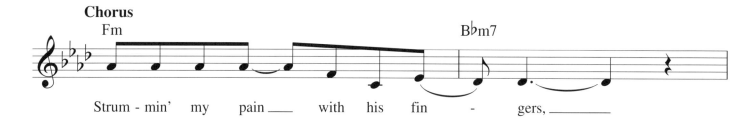

Ah. _____

**Chorus**

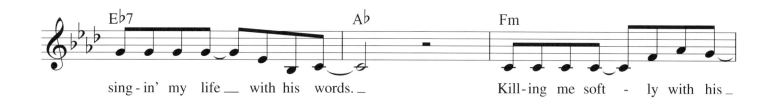

Strum - min' my pain \_\_\_ with his fin - gers, _____

sing - in' my life \_\_ with his words. \_\_ Kill-ing me soft - ly with his \_\_

**Outro-Chorus**

# Midnight Train to Georgia

**Words and Music by Jim Weatherly**

**Verse**

2. He ___ kept dream - in', oo, _____ that some -

day _____ he'd be a star.

But he sure found out the hard ___ way that dreams ___ don't ___ al -

- ways come ___ true. Oh, no. Ah, ah. So he ___

___ pawned all his hopes ___ and he e -

ven sold _____ his old car, mm. Bought a

one - way tick - et back ___ to the life ___ he ___

**Chorus**

Oo, _____ he's leav - in' ___

on the mid - night train ___ to Geor - gia, yeah,

oo, y'all. Said he's go - in' back to find,

oo, ___ a sim - pler place _____ and time, ___ oo, y'all,

ah, ha. I've got to be ___ with him _____

on _____ that ___ mid - night ___ train to Geor - gia, oh, ___

___ ah, ___ hey, ___ hey, ___ hey. I'd rath - er live in his world ___

*Repeat and fade*

**Outro**

than live with-out him in mine. _ *Vocal ad lib. on repeats*

# Neither One of Us
## (Wants to Be the First to Say Goodbye)
### Words and Music by Jim Weatherly

I ___ guess nei - ther one of us

wants to be the first ___ to say, "Good - bye."

**Verse**

2. I _____ keep a - won - der - ing ___

what I'm gon - na do with - out you, and

I guess ___ you must be _____ won - der - ing ___

that same ___ thing, too. ___ So we go

on, go on to - geth - er liv - ing ___

30

_\_\_ a lie _____ be - cause nei-ther one of us_

_wants to be the first \_ to say,_   _"Good - bye."_

**Bridge**

_Ah. _____ Ev -'ry time \_ I find \_ the nerve, \__

_ev - er - y time \_ I find the nerve to say I'm \_\_ leav - ing, _____

_old _____ mem - o - ries, \_\_\_\_\_ those \_ old,_

_old mem-o - ries, \_ they get in my _____ way._   _Ooh. \_\__

_Ah, _____ oh._   _Lord \_ knows it's on - ly \_\_ me,_

and _____ con - vinc - ing our - selves _

to give _ it just _ one ____ more _ try _____

be - cause nei - ther one of us

**Outro**

wants to __ be the first _ to say... Nei - ther one of us

wants to be the first _ to say... _ Ooh. Nei - ther one of us

wants to ___ be ___ the first to say, "Fare - well, _ my _

love, _____ good - bye." _____

# Where Is the Love?

Words and Music by Ralph MacDonald and William Salter

## Pro Vocal® Series
### SONGBOOK & SOUND-ALIKE CD
SING 8 GREAT SONGS
WITH A PROFESSIONAL BAND

Whether you're a karaoke singer or an auditioning professional, the Pro Vocal® series is for you! Unlike most karaoke packs, each book in the Pro Vocal Series contains the lyrics, melody, and chord symbols for eight hit songs. The CD contains demos for listening, and separate backing tracks so you can sing along. The CD is playable on any CD player, but it is also enhanced so PC and Mac computer users can adjust the recording to any pitch without changing the tempo! Perfect for home rehearsal, parties, auditions, corporate events, and gigs without a backup band.

## WOMEN'S EDITIONS

| | | |
|---|---|---|
| 00740409 | **1. Broadway Standards** | $14.95 |
| 00740249 | **2. Jazz Standards** | $14.95 |
| 00740246 | **3. Contemporary Hits** | $14.95 |
| 00740277 | **4. '80s Gold** | $12.95 |
| 00740299 | **5. Christmas Standards** | $15.95 |
| 00740281 | **6. Disco Fever** | $12.95 |
| 00740279 | **7. R&B Super Hits** | $12.95 |
| 00740309 | **8. Wedding Gems** | $12.95 |
| 00740409 | **9. Broadway Standards** | $14.95 |
| 00740348 | **10. Andrew Lloyd Webber** | $14.95 |
| 00740344 | **11. Disney's Best** | $14.95 |
| 00740378 | **12. Ella Fitzgerald** | $14.95 |
| 00740350 | **14. Musicals of Boublil & Schönberg** | $14.95 |
| 00740377 | **15. Kelly Clarkson** | $14.95 |
| 00740377 | **16. Disney Favorites** | $14.95 |
| 00740353 | **17. Jazz Ballads** | $12.95 |
| 00740376 | **18. Jazz Vocal Standards** | $14.95 |
| 00740375 | **20. Hannah Montana** | $16.95 |
| 00740354 | **21. Jazz Favorites** | $12.95 |
| 00740374 | **22. Patsy Cline** | $14.95 |
| 00740369 | **23. Grease** | $14.95 |
| 00740367 | **25. ABBA** | $14.95 |
| 00740365 | **26. Movie Songs** | $14.95 |
| 00740360 | **28. High School Musical 1 & 2** | $14.95 |
| 00740363 | **29. Torch Songs** | $14.99 |
| 00740379 | **30. Hairspray** | $14.95 |
| 00740380 | **31. Top Hits** | $14.95 |
| 00740384 | **32. Hits of the '70s** | $14.95 |
| 00740388 | **33. Billie Holiday** | $14.95 |
| 00740389 | **34. The Sound of Music** | $14.95 |
| 00740390 | **35. Contemporary Christian** | $14.95 |
| 00740392 | **36. Wicked** | $15.99 |
| 00740393 | **37. More Hannah Montana** | $14.95 |
| 00740394 | **38. Miley Cyrus** | $14.95 |
| 00740396 | **39. Christmas Hits** | $15.95 |
| 00740410 | **40. Broadway Classics** | $14.95 |
| 00740415 | **41. Broadway Favorites** | $14.95 |
| 00740416 | **42. Great Standards You Can Sing** | $14.95 |
| 00740417 | **43. Singable Standards** | $14.95 |
| 00740418 | **44. Favorite Standards** | $14.95 |
| 00740419 | **45. Sing Broadway** | $14.95 |
| 00740420 | **46. More Standards** | $14.95 |
| 00740421 | **47. Timeless Hits** | $14.95 |
| 00740422 | **48. Easygoing R&B** | $14.95 |

## MEN'S EDITIONS

| | | |
|---|---|---|
| 00740248 | **1. Broadway Songs** | $14.95 |
| 00740250 | **2. Jazz Standards** | $14.95 |
| 00740251 | **3. Contemporary Hits** | $14.95 |
| 00740278 | **4. '80s Gold** | $12.95 |
| 00740298 | **5. Christmas Standards** | $15.95 |
| 00740280 | **6. R&B Super Hits** | $12.95 |
| 00740282 | **7. Disco Fever** | $12.95 |
| 00740310 | **8. Wedding Gems** | $12.95 |
| 00740411 | **9. Broadway Greats** | $14.95 |
| 00740333 | **10. Elvis Presley – Volume 1** | $14.95 |
| 00740349 | **11. Andrew Lloyd Webber** | $14.95 |
| 00740345 | **12. Disney's Best** | $14.95 |
| 00740347 | **13. Frank Sinatra Classics** | $14.95 |
| 00740334 | **14. Lennon & McCartney** | $14.95 |
| 00740335 | **16. Elvis Presley – Volume 2** | $14.95 |
| 00740343 | **17. Disney Favorites** | $14.95 |
| 00740351 | **18. Musicals of Boublil & Schönberg** | $14.95 |
| 00740346 | **20. Frank Sinatra Standards** | $14.95 |
| 00740362 | **27. Michael Bublé** | $14.95 |
| 00740361 | **28. High School Musical 1 & 2** | $14.95 |
| 00740364 | **29. Torch Songs** | $14.95 |
| 00740366 | **30. Movie Songs** | $14.95 |
| 00740368 | **31. Hip Hop Hits** | $14.95 |
| 00740370 | **32. Grease** | $14.95 |
| 00740371 | **33. Josh Groban** | $14.95 |
| 00740373 | **34. Billy Joel** | $17.95 |
| 00740381 | **35. Hits of the '50s** | $14.95 |
| 00740382 | **36. Hits of the '60s** | $14.95 |
| 00740383 | **37. Hits of the '70s** | $14.95 |
| 00740385 | **38. Motown** | $14.95 |
| 00740386 | **39. Hank Williams** | $14.95 |
| 00740387 | **40. Neil Diamond** | $14.95 |
| 00740391 | **41. Contemporary Christian** | $14.95 |
| 00740397 | **42. Christmas Hits** | $15.95 |
| 00740399 | **43. Ray** | $14.95 |
| 00740400 | **44. The Rat Pack Hits** | $14.95 |
| 00740401 | **45. Songs in the Style of Nat "King" Cole** | $14.95 |
| 00740402 | **46. At the Lounge** | $14.95 |
| 00740403 | **47. The Big Band Singer** | $14.95 |
| 00740404 | **48. Jazz Cabaret Songs** | $14.95 |
| 00740405 | **49. Cabaret Songs** | $14.95 |
| 00740406 | **50. Big Band Standards** | $14.95 |
| 00740412 | **51. Broadway's Best** | $14.95 |

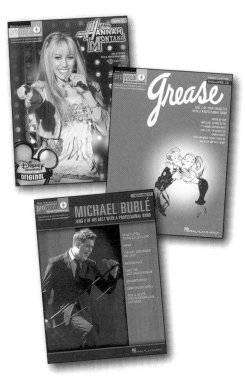

## MIXED EDITIONS

*These editions feature songs for both male and female voices.*

| | | |
|---|---|---|
| 00740311 | **1. Wedding Duets** | $12.95 |
| 00740398 | **2. Enchanted** | $14.95 |
| 00740407 | **3. Rent** | $14.95 |
| 00740408 | **4. Broadway Favorites** | $14.95 |
| 00740413 | **5. South Pacific** | $14.95 |
| 00740414 | **6. High School Musical 3** | $14.95 |

FOR MORE INFORMATION, SEE YOUR LOCAL MUSIC DEALER, OR WRITE TO:

7777 W. BLUEMOUND RD. P.O. BOX 13819 MILWAUKEE, WI 53213

**Visit Hal Leonard online at www.halleonard.com**

Prices, contents, & availability subject to change without notice.
Disney charaters and artwork © Disney Enterprises, Inc.

0109